HOW JOURNALISTS
WORK

BY DUCHESS HARRIS, JD, PHD
WITH LAURA LANE

Core Library

An Imprint of Abdo Publishing

Cover image: Journalists must be able to work in many

abdopublishing.com

Published by Abdo Publishing, a division of ABDO, PO Box 398166, Minneapolis, Minnesota 55439. Copyright © 2018 by Abdo Consulting Group, Inc. International copyrights reserved in all countries. No part of this book may be reproduced in any form without written permission from the publisher. Core Library™ is a trademark and logo of Abdo Publishing.

Printed in the United States of America, North Mankato, Minnesota
102017
012018

THIS BOOK CONTAINS
RECYCLED MATERIALS

Cover Photo: J. Scott Applewhite/AP Images
Interior Photos: J. Scott Applewhite/AP Images, 1; Shutterstock Images, 4–5, 28–29, 30–31, 36–37; Tom Williams/CQ Roll Call/AP Images, 6; A. Katz/Shutterstock Images, 9; Lya Cattel/iStockphoto, 12–13, 43; Jakkrit Orrasri/Shutterstock Images, 15; Red Line Editorial, 16, 38; Samuel Brown/iStockphoto, 20–21; Leonard Zhukovsky/Shutterstock Images, 23; Tashi Delek/iStockphoto, 26; Andy Dean Photography/Shutterstock Images, 41

Editor: Patrick Donnelly
Imprint Designer: Maggie Villaume
Series Design Direction: Megan Anderson

Publisher's Cataloging-in-Publication Data

Names: Harris, Duchess, author. | Lane, Laura, author.
Title: How journalists work / by Duchess Harris and Laura Lane.
Description: Minneapolis, Minnesota : Abdo Publishing, 2018. | Series: News literacy | Includes online resources and index.
Identifiers: LCCN 2017947128 | ISBN 9781532113895 (lib.bdg.) | ISBN 9781532152771 (ebook)
Subjects: LCSH: Reporters and reporting--Juvenile literature. | Journalism--Vocational guidance--Juvenile literature. | Journalism--History--Juvenile literature.
Classification: DDC 071.3--dc23
LC record available at https://lccn.loc.gov/2017947128

CONTENTS

THE JOURNALIST'S ROLE TODAY

Journalist Barbara Ehrenreich has focused her life's work on sharing with people what's happening and why it's important. In 2001 she published an influential book called *Nickel and Dimed.* In it, she exposed the plight of the working poor in the United States.

In her research for the book, Ehrenreich went undercover and worked as a waitress, hotel maid, house cleaner, nursing home aide, and Walmart salesperson. Ehrenreich found these jobs to be mentally and physically exhausting. She discovered that many

Reporters work hard to meet their deadlines.

Author Barbara Ehrenreich moderates a press conference on the effects of the economic crisis in April 2009.

Americans working in these low-paying jobs had to have two or three jobs to survive. Ehrenreich did not simply want to describe the plight of the working poor. She wanted to help improve their working conditions and pay. She said, "As a journalist, I search for the truth. But as a moral person, I am also obliged to do something about it."

CAN ANYONE BE A JOURNALIST?

Journalists gather information, create a story about it, and share that story with the public. Some journalists write stories for people to read in newspapers or magazines or on the Internet. Others record audio or video reports for people to listen to on the radio or watch on television. Journalists go by different names, including reporters and correspondents.

Anyone can gather information and share it with the world. People can write articles and publish their work on blogs. People can take photos and videos on smartphones and post them online. But there are differences between journalists and citizens acting as journalists. The job of journalists is to report news stories. They are paid to do it.

THE DOWNFALL OF A PRESIDENT

On August 9, 1974, the front-page headline of the *Washington Post* said simply, "Nixon Resigns." Richard Nixon was president of the United States. He was forced to give up his job. He had been part of the Watergate scandal. He knew about a plot to break into his political opponents' offices in the Watergate building in Washington, DC. Journalists found out what happened. They wrote stories about it. Citizens read newspaper articles and watched television reports about what had happened. The public believed Nixon lied. Nixon became very unpopular and decided to resign.

Journalists must get the facts straight. Editors check their work before it's published. Journalists can lose their jobs if they make mistakes.

Citizens acting as journalists are not being paid to report stories. No one reviews their work or makes sure they get the facts right. They most likely do not have the same education and training that a journalist does. Their contributions can be valuable, however. They might be on the scene of a newsworthy event before reporters can arrive. In those cases, citizens

In 2011, protesters marched in New York City for Occupy Wall Street.

can provide the first reports to help tell a story from another perspective.

BECOMING A JOURNALIST

Journalists usually graduate from a four-year college program. While in college, students might study journalism, communications, English, or political science. Students are also encouraged to get real-world experience. College students might work for a news organization in a position called an internship. After the internship, students can show employers samples of their best print, audio, or video news stories.

One of the biggest challenges journalists face is keeping up with technology. Before personal computers became standard, a print journalist's main tools were a pen, a notebook, and a typewriter.

Today, journalists must be good at communicating in not just one medium but in many—print, audio, and video. Now, before heading out to cover a story, a reporter must make several decisions: "Should I take a digital camcorder, camera, or audio recorder? Should I search for what other people are saying about the topic online now or later? Should I post a quick update on social media?"

In a survey, more than 68 percent of journalists said they would like additional training to cope with these new job expectations. Journalists want more training in social media skills, as well as in shooting and editing video.

STRAIGHT TO THE
SOURCE

Americans' freedoms have been protected by the US Constitution and the Bill of Rights since the documents were ratified by the states in 1791. The First Amendment to the Constitution covers the many ways that we choose to express ourselves, including through the media. Drafted by James Madison, the First Amendment states:

> *Congress shall make no law respecting an establishment of religion, or prohibiting the free exercise thereof; or abridging the freedom of speech, or of the press; or the right of the people peaceably to assemble, and to petition the Government for a redress of grievances.*

> Source: "The Bill of Rights: A Transcription." *America's Founding Documents*. National Archives, June 26, 2017. Web. Accessed September 13, 2017.

What's the Big Idea?

Take a close look at this passage. What freedoms does the First Amendment give to citizens of the United States? Why was it important to citizens to have these freedoms added to the Constitution? Is there a difference between freedom of speech and freedom of the press?

GATHERING NEWS

Journalists find stories to report on. They might get tips on stories from people in the community. They might find a story idea on the Internet. Their editors can also assign them stories to cover.

Journalists don't have time to report on everything that is happening. Working with their editors, they must choose which stories to share with the public. Some stories are more important or interesting than others.

Most reporters hope to "get the scoop." This means they are the first to report the story to the public. Journalists often race to be the

Reporters race to the scene so they can grab the first interviews and film the first footage for a new story.

first one to get a story in print or on the air. But getting the story right is more important than being first. A journalist wants to be a trusted source of information for people.

GETTING THE FACTS STRAIGHT

Journalists must report accurate information. Journalists use multiple sources when gathering information. They check and recheck facts to make sure they're getting the story right. Journalists also quote people in stories. A journalist tells readers who said what. This way readers know who journalists interviewed to get the story.

INTERVIEWING EXPERTS

Journalists often interview experts. Experts are people who have in-depth knowledge in a subject area. Journalists can find experts by typing in their topic on an Internet search engine. They can look at who is writing articles or doing studies on their topic. For example, university professors are experts in their fields of study. A journalist could interview an astronomy professor about the discovery of a new planet.

Reporters often interview athletes and coaches after games.

Readers expect journalists to talk to people who are knowledgeable about the story.

COVERING A BEAT

Reporters often cover a "beat." Covering a beat means focusing on one particular area. Different beats include education, sports, business, entertainment, local news,

BEATS JOURNALISTS COVER

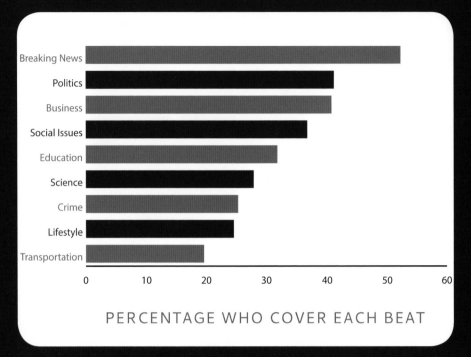

PERCENTAGE WHO COVER EACH BEAT

Journalists cover many beats, often at the same time. One survey asked reporters which beats they cover most often. This chart shows the results. Why do you think some beats are covered more than others?

and government. Journalists get to know people on their beat. For example, a reporter who is covering sports in a small town might get to know the high school football coach and players. She can ask them questions before and after games to get information for her reports.

INTERVIEWING SOURCES

Journalists must learn about the topics they are covering. Their work often begins with gathering background information. They can research their topics in newspapers, books, and magazines. They can use the Internet for research too.

Reporters then interview people who have information about a topic or event. Journalists ask about what happened. They ask about who was involved. They need to know when and where something happened.

IN THE REAL WORLD

JOURNALISTS AS DETECTIVES

In an interview, James T. Hamilton, a professor of journalism at Stanford University and the author of *Democracy's Detectives: The Economics of Investigative Journalism*, said it can be expensive to investigate a story. The higher price can be worth it, though. Journalists can reveal when something dishonest is happening. Then the public can demand things change for the better. Hamilton said, "For each dollar invested in an investigative story, there can be over $100 in benefits to society."

They also need to know why and how something occurred. Journalists can write down answers. They can also record the interview. After an interview, the journalist reviews her notes. If she needs more information, she can contact the person again.

Reporters also gather information at news conferences. A news conference is an interview by a group of journalists. Politicians or sports figures might hold news conferences to address questions once rather than having to repeat their responses to the same question from multiple reporters.

INVESTIGATING

While doing research, a journalist might discover something dishonest is happening. The people involved might want to keep what's going on a secret. The journalist must dig deeper to uncover more information about the story. The Internet is a powerful tool that helps journalists search for information. A journalist can also ask to see government records or reports.

A journalist's investigative work can make a difference. For example, Pat Stith, a reporter for the *News & Observer* in Raleigh, North Carolina, reported on more than 300 investigations he conducted between 1966 and 2008. During that time, 31 new laws were passed in North Carolina to address issues that Stith's work uncovered. They include regulations covering the environment, public safety, health care, civil rights, and criminal justice.

FURTHER EVIDENCE

Chapter Two has quite a bit of information about how journalists gather news before writing a story. What was one of the main points of this chapter? What key evidence supports this point? Go to the article about journalism at the website below. Find a quote from the website that supports the main point you identified. Does the quote support an existing piece of evidence in the chapter? Or does it offer a new piece of evidence?

WHAT IS JOURNALISM?
abdocorelibrary.com/how-journalists-work

CHAPTER
THREE

WRITING THE STORY

After gathering news, a journalist must write the story. Reporters work with editors to tailor the story to the audience. For example, if a story is being published in print, the journalist must write for the eye. The reporter might use short paragraphs. Editors add photos to illustrate the text. This makes the story more informative and easier to read.

If a story is broadcast on radio or television, the journalist writes the story for the ear. The story is short. The journalist writes

A reporter writes her story after gathering all of her information.

the story as if he is talking with the listener or viewer.

THE FIVE Ws AND THE H

The first paragraph of a news story is called a lede. The lede is the most important part of the story. It must grab the readers' attention or they might not read the rest of the story. In the first and second paragraphs, a reporter should try to cover the "Five Ws and the H:" who, what, why, where, when, and how the story happened. The less important details follow after the opening paragraphs.

A CBS Channel 2 News van drives in New York City.

Sometimes journalists take another approach. They begin a story with an anecdote. An anecdote is a short, interesting story within the larger story. Imagine that a journalist is covering the opening of a new baseball stadium. The reporter might interview a fan who is old enough to remember when the team's last new stadium opened. The reporter might compare the price of tickets or concessions to show how much has changed over the years. The fan might also talk about the excitement that accompanied the opening of each stadium.

THE ROLE OF BIAS

Journalists strive to be fair and accurate. This is not always easy. Journalists are citizens too. They have their own ideas and opinions about what is happening in the world. It is the job of journalists to keep their own opinions separate from the story they are telling.

Journalists make choices when telling a story. They choose which facts to include. They choose which facts to leave out. They decide how to arrange the facts in the story. People can disagree with a journalist's story. They might say the story is not fair. They may think the journalist did not report both sides accurately. They may accuse him of bias, or allowing his opinion to affect how the story is reported.

MEETING DEADLINES

Journalism is a demanding profession. The work is fast-paced and competitive. Journalists work under deadlines. A deadline is the time when a journalist must finish a story and turn it in. Reporters are out in the field interviewing sources. They are investigating what happened. Journalists are under pressure to be the first to report important stories.

News can happen at any time. Journalists might have to work nights and weekends. They also might have to change their schedules to cover breaking news. Thanks to the Internet, reporters can publish what they know about a story immediately, rather than

EXPLORE ONLINE

Chapter Three talks about the process journalists use when writing a news story. The video at the website below goes into more depth on this topic. How is the information from the video the same as the information in Chapter Three? What new information did you learn from this video?

BEYOND THE FRONT PAGE—TELLING THE STORY
abdocorelibrary.com/how-journalists-work

having to wait until the evening news or the next day's newspaper. They can share information about the story as it evolves over time until their final story is ready for publication. With the pressure to get information out quickly, however, journalists can struggle to get the facts straight. Journalists must balance the demand to get the story out first with their duty to report accurate information.

A news anchor delivers breaking news in a television broadcast.

CHAPTER
FOUR

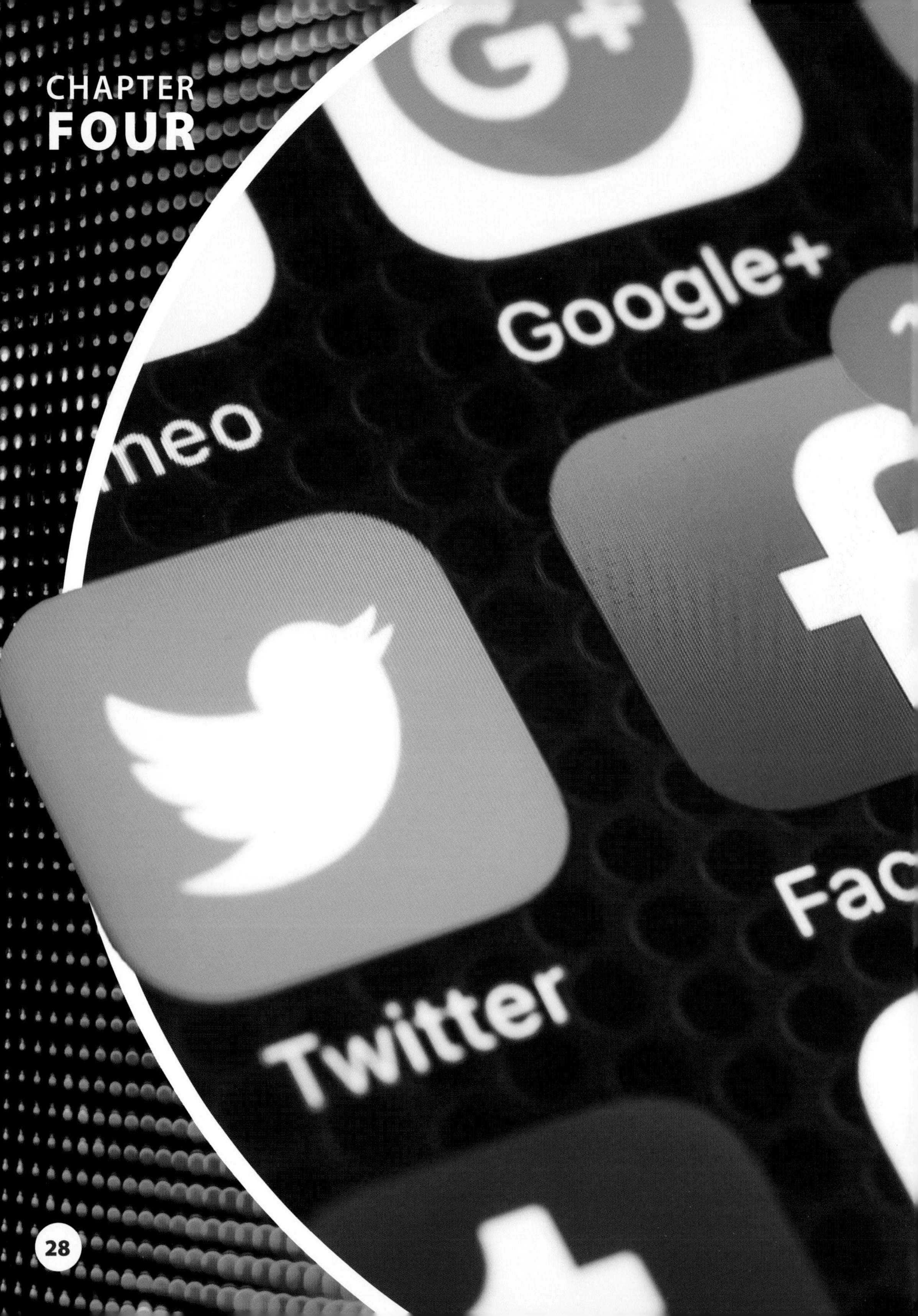

PUBLISHING THE STORY

Americans are flooded with information. Most of this information is not news. In one study of social media, researchers reported that almost 99 percent of the information posted on that platform was "pointless babble," not essential news. A journalist's story needs to be interesting and easy to read. It must cut through the noise and stand out from the crowd.

WORKING WITH EDITORS

Editors review stories. Journalists work with editors to make sure their stories are accurate

Americans get their news through a variety of social media and other Internet outlets.

A newspaper rack carries a variety of newspapers, often from all over the world.

and well written. An editor may ask a journalist to go back and rewrite a story or change parts of it.

There are different types of editors. Newspaper editors review the grammar, punctuation, and spelling in

a story. They may check facts, dates, and statistics. Copy editors might also write headlines and design page layouts. They will decide where stories, photos, and ads are placed on each page.

SEVEN ELEMENTS
OF A GOOD STORY

Award-winning journalist Donald M. Murray said a good story needs seven things. First, a story must have information. Second, that information must be important to readers. Third, a story should be focused. Fourth, a story should be put in context. This means the journalist gives readers background information to help understand the topic better. Fifth, a story needs people. People like to read about other people. Sixth, a story must be well organized. And finally, a story must have a voice. It should read as if the journalist is talking aloud to the reader.

Assistant editors might focus on a particular area such as local news or sports. They can share in the duties of assigning stories to journalists. In many newsrooms, the executive editor oversees the entire operation. The executive editor has the final say about what stories are published.

READY TO PUBLISH!

Once editors have approved a story, it is ready to be published. The story will be available for many people to read, listen to, or watch on television. The Internet also plays a role in the publishing process. Newspapers, radio stations, and television stations have websites on which they publish stories. Journalists can post stories on websites immediately. They can combine written stories with audio and video. Journalists can also link readers to additional sources of information. People can also download audio programs known as podcasts from the Internet and listen to the audio material whenever they want.

The Internet is interactive. Readers can post comments about a story they have read. Journalists can respond to the readers' comments. Readers and journalists can have a conversation online. For example, in *The Online Journalism Handbook*, one reporter described how a company went bankrupt, and the new owner would not take the previous owner's gift cards. People were angry and asked the newspaper's staff to investigate. On the newspaper's blog, reporters

THE VALUE OF COPYEDITING

Fred Vultee, an associate professor at Wayne State University, conducted a study to determine the value of copyediting. Vultee asked participants to read edited stories and unedited stories. The participants said the edited stories were more professional, better organized, and better written than the stories that had not been edited. The participants said they were willing to pay for stories that had been edited.

posted daily updates every time they called the new owner and indicated whether or not the new owner had answered them. Eventually, one of the reporters got an interview with the company's new owner. The entire interview was posted on the newspaper's website. Another reporter from a different organization saw it, and the journalists shared information with each other. Readers also posted links to other stories on the topic from other news organizations.

STRAIGHT TO THE
SOURCE

The relationship between a journalist and an editor can be difficult. The journalist might disagree with the changes an editor makes to a story. In the excerpt below, reporter and author Donald M. Murray described how he felt about working with editors.

> *When I first started writing, I thought editors were my enemy, but eventually I learned that I needed editors. Editors allowed me to be more daring, to attempt to write what I have not written before in ways that might not work, and I learned that few writers ever thank editors, instead taking their byline and dancing alone in front of the reader. When assigning or copyeditors help me, I thank them after we talk or in a note—and when they help me frequently, a note goes to their editors.*

> Source: Donald M. Murray. *Writing to Deadline: The Journalist at Work*. Portsmouth, NH: Heinemann, 2000. Print. 178.

Point of View

As a young journalist, what was Murray's view of working with editors? Why did his opinion change over time? Read back through this chapter. Do you think journalists need editors to review their stories?

CHAPTER
FIVE

THE AUDIENCE

The audience is made up of the people who read, listen to, or watch a journalist's work. Journalists shape stories to fit their audience's needs. This way they can write stories people find interesting and useful. Sometimes, rather than appealing to an audience's interests, a journalist might report on a story that will be important to the audience, even if it knows very little about the subject.

THE ROLE OF THE INTERNET AND SOCIAL MEDIA

The Internet has changed the way journalists reach their audiences. Journalists can post stories on websites immediately. They don't

Mobile devices help today's journalists reach a broader audience.

NEWS
TRENDS

In a study conducted by the Pew Research Center, young adults said they are less interested in news than older adults. When young adults follow news, they find the media less trustworthy than older people do. Why might young adults trust news less than older adults do?

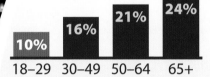

TRUST INFORMATION FROM THE NATIONAL MEDIA

18–29: 10%
30–49: 16%
50–64: 21%
65+: 24%

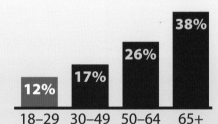

SAY NATIONAL MEDIA DOES A VERY GOOD JOB KEEPING THEM INFORMED

18–29: 12%
30–49: 17%
50–64: 26%
65+: 38%

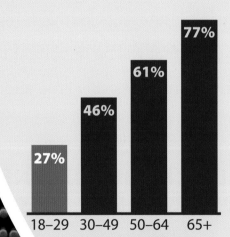

FOLLOW NEWS ALL OR MOST OF THE TIME

18–29: 27%
30–49: 46%
50–64: 61%
65+: 77%

have to wait for a newspaper to be printed the next day. They don't have to wait for a television show to air hours later.

Social media is an important tool journalists use in their work. Social media includes websites on which people can create and share content. The content can include text, audio clips, or videos. People can also interact with other people on social media sites.

THE 24-HOUR CABLE NEWS CYCLE

In 1980 Ted Turner and his business partners launched the Cable News Network (CNN). CNN broadcasts news 24 hours a day. CNN was the first network that could use satellite signals to cover news happening around the globe. Americans could watch events unfolding live on CNN. For example, Americans watched the United States military sending missiles into Iraq at the start of the Persian Gulf War (1991). Former president Bill Clinton said, "When some emergency happens somewhere in the world, there's a 50-50 chance I can look at it on CNN quicker than I can get a report from the State Department."

THE DECLINE OF NEWSPAPERS

Over the past two decades, major newspapers have seen a sharp decrease in revenue. Rupert Murdoch, the head of the global for-profit News Corporation, told editors that in order to counter that trend, newspapers must adapt to the Internet. Murdoch said, "The challenge for us . . . is to create an Internet presence that is compelling enough for users to make us their home page. Just as people traditionally started their day with coffee and the newspaper, in the future, our hope should be that for those who start their day online, it will be with coffee and our website."

Journalists rely on social media to keep up with breaking news. It became especially important to monitor Twitter after Donald Trump was elected president. Early in his presidency, Trump often used Twitter to communicate directly with his followers. He sometimes used it to communicate policy changes. Reporters then had to react quickly to investigate any new information contained in his tweets.

CNN reports on the outcome of the 2016 presidential election.

One example came in July 2017, when Trump tweeted that transgender people would be banned from serving in the US military. Reporters then had to scramble to reach sources and get comments or information for their stories reacting to the tweet.

Despite the many challenges journalists face in the Internet age, their goals remain simple. They must be able to gather information and accurately communicate a story to their audience. Journalists help keep citizens informed so they can make good decisions. In this way, a journalist's work is essential to a free society.

FAST FACTS

- Journalists are storytellers.

- The purpose of a journalist's work is to give people accurate information about what is happening in the world outside, not to produce stories fast.

- Journalists share stories with people in newspapers and magazines, on the Internet, on the radio, or on television.

- Journalists keep an eye on what the government is doing and tell people about it.

- Most journalists graduate from four-year college programs.

- Journalists often cover a beat such as education, sports, or local news.

- Journalists can cover local, national, or international news.

- Journalists interview people who have information about a topic or event.

- Sometimes journalists must investigate or dig deeper to uncover more information about a story.

- Journalists work under deadlines.

- Social media is an important tool that many journalists use in their reporting.

STOP AND THINK

Tell the Tale

Chapter Three discusses how journalists write stories. Imagine you are a reporter for your school newspaper. Your class is holding an election for class president. What kinds of questions would you ask the candidates in an interview? What issues are important to you and to the overall student body?

Surprise Me

Chapter Two discusses how journalists gather news. After reading this book, what two or three facts about how journalists work did you find most surprising? Write a few sentences about each fact. Why did you find each fact surprising?

Dig Deeper

After reading this book, what questions do you still have about how journalists do their work? With an adult's help, find a few reliable sources that can help you answer your questions. Write a paragraph about what you learned.

GLOSSARY

anecdote
a short, interesting story

beat
a particular area a journalist
focuses on, such as local
news, education, or sports

bias
prejudice in favor of or
against an idea or person

correspondents
another word for journalists

deadline
the date and time an
assignment is due

editor
a journalist who works with
reporters to improve their
stories before publication

internship
a position that allows
a college student to
work in a job field to
gain experience

interview
a conversation between two
people in which one person
asks questions and the other
person answers them

social media
websites on which people
create and share content and
interact with other people

ONLINE
RESOURCES

To learn more about how journalists work, visit our free resource websites below.

Visit **abdocorelibrary.com** for free Common Core resources for teachers and students, including vetted activities, multimedia, and booklinks, for deeper subject comprehension.

Visit **abdobooklinks.com** for free additional online weblinks for further learning. These links are routinely monitored and updated to provide the most current information available.

LEARN
MORE

Christensen, Bonnie. *The Daring Nellie Bly: America's Star Reporter.* New York: Dragonfly, 2009.

Gitlin, Marty. *Joseph Pulitzer: Historic Newspaper Publisher.* Minneapolis, MN: Abdo Publishing, 2010.

ABOUT THE
AUTHORS

Duchess Harris, JD, PhD
Professor Harris is the chair of the American Studies Department at Macalester College. The author and coauthor of four books (*Hidden Human Computers: The Black Women of NASA* and *Black Lives Matter* with Sue Bradford Edwards, *Racially Writing the Republic: Racists, Race Rebels, and Transformations of American Identity* with Bruce Baum, and *Black Feminist Politics from Kennedy to Clinton/Obama*), she has been an associate editor for *Litigation News*, the American Bar Association Section's quarterly flagship publication, and was the first editor-in-chief of *Law Raza Journal*, an interactive online race and the law journal for William Mitchell College of Law.

She has earned a PhD in American Studies from the University of Minnesota and a Juris Doctorate from William Mitchell College of Law.

Laura Lane

Laura Lane lives in Wisconsin with her husband and two children. She enjoys writing about social studies and science for children. She worked as a journalist for a newspaper after college.

INDEX